AMAZING MISSOURI ANIMALS

MAMMALS, BIRDS, REPTILES, AND MO!

CAROLYN MUELLER KELLY

REEDY PRESS

For my dad, who loves Missouri's rivers and lakes and taught his children and grandchildren to do the same.

Reedy Press
PO Box 5131
St. Louis, MO 63139
reedypress.com

Library of Congress Control Number: 2025948566

ISBN: 9781681065991

Design by Richard Roden

Cover photos: Missouri fox trotter photo by Kayla Oakes/
Wikimedia Commons
https://commons.wikimedia.org/w/index.php?curid=12602351
Rattlesnake photo by Peter Paplanus/Wikimedia Commons
https://commons.wikimedia.org/wiki/File:Timber_Rattlesnake_(Crotalus_horridus)_(31140366037).jpg
Spring peeper photo by Judy Gallagher/Wikimedia Commons
https://commons.wikimedia.org/w/index.php?curid=66901841

All images are courtesy of the author or believed to be in the public domain unless noted otherwise.

Printed in Canada

26 27 28 29 30 5 4 3 2 1

CONTENTS

Introduction 4
Words to Know and Love 7
Black Bears 8
Pumas 11
Opossums 13
Coyotes 14
Beavers 16
Woodchucks 19
Squirrels 21
Moles 22
Spring Peepers 24
Hellbenders 27
Copperheads 29
Cottonmouths 30
Rattlesnakes 33
Snapping Turtles 34
Box Turtles 37
Tiger Salamanders 38
Eastern Bluebirds 41
Great Horned Owls 42
Snowy Egrets 45
Turkey Vultures 46
Mules 49
Jim the Wonder Dog 51
Lily the Search and Rescue Dog 52
Maverick the Great Dane 55
Bobcats 57
White-Tailed Deer 59
North American River Otters 60
Spiny Softshell Turtles 62
Greater Prairie Chickens 65
Burying Beetles 66
Missouri Fox Trotters 68
Old Drum the Dog 71
Anna the Mexican Wolf 72
Paddlefish 75
Channel Catfish 76
Crayfish 79
Wild Horses 80
Bald Eagles 83
Prairie Racerunner Lizards 84
Alligator Gar 87
Raccoons 89
Peanut the Turtle 91
Bats 92
Nine-Banded Armadillo 94
Where to Visit and Learn About Animals in Missouri 96

INTRODUCTION

I spent my childhood in suburban St. Louis, with a little patch of woods behind our home. Every summer, box turtles wandered into our grassy yard. Black-and-yellow garter snakes startled us, slithering underfoot. If we were lucky, we might glimpse a barred owl swooping silently through the dusk, or a flock of turkeys pecking along their merry way. Deer were a mainstay. They easily hopped the backyard fence, a flash of white from their tails. Some magical mornings a doe tiptoed through with her freckled fawns. And then, there were the coyotes. They howled me to sleep most nights, synchronizing their chorus with nearby sirens, or appeared in the morning hours, trotting warily on the edge of the woods. Their presence thrilled me, scared me, and sparked my imagination all at once, igniting a lifelong love and respect for wild things.

All of these animals were a mere 15 miles from downtown St. Louis.

Missouri is full of remarkable wildlife. From bobcats and burying beetles to crayfish and copperheads, no matter where you live, there's much to see and explore. This book celebrates a sampling of our amazing Missouri animals. You can use it as a field guide while exploring Missouri's woods, streams, and prairies, or even your own backyard. You'll meet some of our state's animal heroes, like Maverick the Great Dane and Jim the Wonder Dog. But most importantly, you'll learn about some of our very special species and what makes each one unique.

In my teenage years, a subdivision was built behind our house, cutting significantly into the woods of my childhood. Gradually, coyote sightings became rare, and their howls disappeared from the nocturnal soundscape entirely. Wild things need their wild places. And it's up to all of us to encourage the amazing animals in our state by protecting our land and keeping our rivers clean. The generations reading this book are the future stewards of Missouri's diverse habitats. The first step toward stewardship is learning as much as you can about what you are trying to protect. It is my hope that this book will act as a primer for budding biologists and citizen scientists who want to learn all about the furred, fanged, and finned creatures that call Missouri home.

My love of wildlife started with a coyote. But for you, it might be a bluebird, a snapping turtle, a hellbender, or a mole. Senegalese forestry engineer Baba Dioum famously said, "In the end, we will conserve only what we love, we will love only what we understand, and we will understand only what we are taught." Missourians put it much more simply . . . show me. I hope that you find inspiration in these pages and a love for our state's remarkable wildlife as you embark on your own journey to see and understand Missouri's amazing animals.

Courtesy of NPS

Photo by Chris Ensminger on Unsplash

WORDS TO KNOW AND LOVE

Carnivore: Animals that eat meat

Herbivore: Animals that eat plants

Omnivore: Animals that eat both meat and plants

Insectivore: Animals that primarily eat insects

Oviparous: Producing young by laying eggs

Ovoviviparous: Producing young by means of eggs that are hatched within the body of the parent who then gives birth to live young

Viviparous: Producing live young that have developed within the body of the parent

Ectotherm: An animal that regulates its body temperature from external sources

Endotherm: An animal that regulates its body temperature internally

Spawning: When an animal releases or deposits eggs

Endemic: When an animal is native to a certain place

Hibernation: A state of dormancy that some animals enter during the winter to conserve energy

Scat: A scientific word for poop

Marsupial: The group of mammals commonly thought of as "pouched mammals"

Conspecifics: Members of the same species

Inorganic: Naturally occurring substances that are not from living things

Organic: Derived from living organisms

Fertilize: To develop a new individual by introducing male genetic material

Juvenile: A young animal

Cloaca: An all-purpose hole or common cavity in animals that can be used for both digestive and reproductive purposes

Carapace: The top part of a turtle's shell

Plastron: The bottom part of a turtle's shell

Cutaneous respiration: Gas exchange directly through the skin of an animal

Metamorphosis/metamorphosed: A biological process where an animal undergoes a dramatic transformation

Apex predators: Animals at the top of the food chain

Hybrid: The offspring of two animals who are each a different species

Diurnal: Active in the daytime

Nocturnal: Active in the nighttime

Crepuscular: Active at dawn and dusk

Prey: Animals that other animals eat

Predator: Animals that eat other animals

Mustelids: A family of carnivorous animals that includes weasels, badgers, otters, polecats, and wolverines

Ecosystem: All of the living things (animals, plants, organisms) in a given area interacting with each other and their nonliving environment

Carrion: Dead animals

Rostrum: A snoutlike protrusion

Broods: Groups of chicks

External fertilization: A reproductive process where the fusion of egg and sperm occurs outside the parents' bodies, typically in an aquatic environment

BLACK BEARS

There are eight species of bear in the world, and we are lucky to have three of them in North America. One species is endemic to Missouri—the black bear! Though these bears can have brown, cream, white, or cinnamon coats, they are most commonly black, earning their name. Before western settlers moved into Missouri, black bears were abundant. In the pioneer era, they were hunted for food and pelts. By 1931, black bears were thought to be extinct in Missouri. In the 21st century, however, bears have begun to reappear—with a healthy population that has grown to around 900 bears. Black bears are one of the largest mammals in Missouri. They are omnivores, just like we are, so they like to eat pretty much anything you like to eat and then some—unless you like to eat grubs, crickets, and carrion, which, you know, no judgment. Another classic bear trope that holds true for black bears? Hibernation*. These bears hibernate through the winter in dens or caves. In the spring, mothers and cubs emerge from their dens together to explore their world. Here's another stereotype about bears that is absolutely true: You don't want to mess with a mama bear, so if you see a bear with cubs, steer clear!

Scientific Name: *Ursus americanus* ("American bear")

Order: Carnivora

Family: Ursidae

Population: Around 900

Region: Most are found south of the Missouri River, but some have been seen as far north as the Iowa border.

Diet: Omnivorous (grasses, plants, fruits, berries, nuts, insects, honey, roots, fish, frogs, birds, small mammals, eggs, fawns, and carrion)

Scientifically referred to as "torpor" but known as "hibernation" in common culture. Only a few animals (like woodchucks) are true hibernators.

Photo by TheOtherKev

MISSOURI'S BLACK BEAR POPULATION IS GROWING. MOST OF THE BEARS LIVE IN THE SOUTHERN THIRD OF THE STATE, ESCECIALLY THE OZARKS.

Photo by Dylan Crawford on Unsplash

PUMAS

Puma. Cougar. Mountain lion. Panther. Catamount. A cat by any other name would smell as sweet—though you should not try to get close enough to find out! Pumas go by lots of different names, depending on the area of the world and culture. But their scientific name is *Puma concolor*, so we'll stick with "puma." Though rare in Missouri, pumas are the largest and most widely dispersed cat species found in North America. Because they lack the specialized vocal folds and larynx of cats like lions and tigers and cannot roar, they are not technically classified as "big cats." Though they are famous for their high-pitched "scream!" Like all cats, pumas are elusive hunters. Even in areas where pumas are common, they are seldom seen. Instead, cats leave a "calling card" in the form of scat, tracks, scrapes, and remnants of kills. Pumas, like other cats, are obligate carnivores, meaning that unlike Missouri's black bears, they will eat only meat. This meat can come in the form of any bird or mammal, ranging from small rodents to deer. In fact, the current century's prevalence of deer in Missouri can be attributed to a decline in apex predators like pumas. The athletic brand Puma is named after this species for good reason. These animals are extremely athletic, sprinting at speeds up to 50 miles per hour and leaping vertically up to 18 feet!

OF THE CONFIRMED SIGHTINGS, ONLY TWO FEMALES HAVE BEEN DOCUMENTED.

Scientific Name: *Puma concolor* (*Puma* is the South American name for this animal; *concolor* translates to "of uniform color.")

Order: Carnivora

Family: Felidae

Status: An average of eight sightings a year since the mid-2000s

Region: Sightings scattered statewide, but no documented breeding population

Diet: Carnivorous (deer, small mammals, and birds)

Photo by Thomas S. on Unsplash

OPOSSUMS ARE THE ONLY MARSUPIAL NATIVE TO NORTH AMERICA.

OPOSSUMS

Opossums get a bad rap. Lots of Missourians look down on opossums, seeing them merely as roadkill, garbage eaters, or, because of their naked tails, giant rats. These stereotypes keep people from celebrating one of Missouri's most amazing animals! Australia is famous for its marsupials, but in the US, the opossum is the only native marsupial. This means that opossum babies—called joeys—are born very underdeveloped, barely larger than a honeybee. They are born into their mother's pouch, where they stay, drinking her milk and getting bigger and stronger, until they are old enough to leave the pouch and explore the world at around two months old. At this point, the joeys ride on their mother's back. A female can have up to 25 babies in a litter, but because she has only 13 teats, only a handful of them will survive. Opossums are a dentist's dream—they have 50 teeth, more than any other land mammal! And that ratlike tail that gives them their not-so-great reputation? Their tails are semi-prehensile, which means that they can wrap them around things to help them grasp objects. Though you may see it in the comics, an opossum can't actually hang from its tail. It's not truly prehensile and can't fully support its weight. But it still lends a hand . . . er, tail . . . to these tree-loving critters while they climb.

FEMALES CAN HAVE TWO TO THREE LITTERS PER YEAR.

Scientific Name: *Didelphidae virginiana* ("New World marsupials from Virginia")

Order: Didelphimorphia

Family: Didelphidae

Status: Common

Region: Statewide

Diet: Omnivorous (insects, carrion, reptiles, amphibians, crayfish, birds, eggs, worms, fruits, and . . . garbage)

COYOTES

Coyotes are a mammal that has thrived alongside our human communities. Coyotes live throughout the state, in rural, suburban, and urban areas. A pack of coyotes has even been documented breeding in St. Louis's Forest Park! Coyotes are members of the canid family, meaning that they are closely related to animals like wolves, foxes, and dogs. Like other canids, coyotes are not true dietary carnivores. Instead, they are technically omnivores and eat a fairly diverse diet. They will sometimes eat fruits or berries, seeds, or grasses, but their preferred prey are small mammals like rabbits and mice. A characteristic of the coyote that gives them a bad rap is their infamous howl. It's hard to miss a pack of coyotes howling. Their signature "ahahahwoooooooo!" sounds can be heard for up to a mile. But these eerie calls aren't evil. Coyote howls can be used to bond with their family group or to broadcast their territory to conspecifics. Once one group of coyotes starts howling, others in the area will often join in. Even if these animals might sound scary, they're not very big, and definitely not bad. Their songs are hauntingly beautiful and are a natural part of Missouri's nocturnal soundscape.

Scientific Name: *Canis latrans* ("barking dog")

Order: Carnivora

Family: Canidae

Status: Common

Region: Common throughout the state but most abundant in grasslands of northern and western Missouri

Diet: Omnivorous (small mammals, deer, some plants, and carrion)

BOTH COYOTE PARENTS TAKE CARE OF THEIR PUPS. MALE COYOTES HELP FEED AND PROTECT THEM.

BEAVERS

When most people think of rodents, images of rats and mice come to mind. But there are lots of species in the order Rodentia, including the beaver! Beavers are well-known for felling trees with their giant front incisors and then using these trees to dam rivers. They have the ability to shape the landscape around them. In Missouri, beavers don't usually build true dams. Because our state is home to faster, fluctuating streams, Missouri's beavers typically dig out bankside dens with an underwater entrance. In extremely cold climates, beavers will spend months at a time living entirely under the ice in their lodges. When Missouri was first settled by Europeans, many areas were populated by fur trappers. Beaver pelts were prized in the fur-trapping business, nearly eradicating the species from the state. Conservation efforts have now created a sustainable beaver population, and these little loggers—or evidence of them—can be seen along many riverways or wetlands. Like all rodents, a beaver's incisors grow throughout its life. But unlike most other rodents, a beaver's front teeth are bright orange!

BEAVERS PREFER AREAS WITH SOFTWOOD TREES LIKE WILLOW AND COTTONWOOD FOR THEIR FOOD AND BUILDING MATERIALS.

Scientific Name: *Castor canadensis* ("beaver from Canada")

Order: Rodentia

Family: Castoridae

Status: Common

Region: Statewide along waterways

Diet: Herbivorous (barks and woody vegetation, plants, lilies, and herbaceous plants)

WOODCHUCK BURROWS CAN BE 15 TO 25 FEET LONG HORIZONTALLY, WITH MULTIPLE ENTRANCES.

WOODCHUCKS

Speaking of rodents . . . consider the woodchuck. How much wood would a woodchuck chuck if a woodchuck could chuck wood? Well, the answer is, it "woodn't." (See what I did there?) Woodchucks are not named for the ability to chuck wood. Their name is derived from the Algonquin word *wuchak*, which means "digger." Now, this is an appropriate name because these small mammals are excellent diggers, moving almost three tons of dirt when preparing their burrows. Like the puma, woodchucks go by a lot of different names, including groundhog, whistle pig (my personal favorite), land beaver, and thick woods badger. But these animals are not pigs, beavers, or badgers. They are technically squirrels. Woodchucks are North America's largest ground squirrel, and they are prevalent in Missouri. Most people know a bit about the biology of a woodchuck thanks to the tradition of Groundhog Day. Every year on February 2, the world's most famous groundhog, Punxsutawney Phil, emerges from his burrow in Pennsylvania and predicts the coming weather. Though it's a strange tradition, it is true that woodchucks are some of the world's only true hibernators. In winter months, when they are denned up in their burrows, woodchucks can lower their body temperature to 38 degrees Fahrenheit, and their heart beats a mere four times per minute. Whether or not Phil sees his shadow, woodchucks emerging from their burrows in Missouri are a sure sign of spring!

Scientific Name: *Marmota monax* ("digger" or "solitary ground squirrel")

Order: Rodentia

Family: Sciuridae

Status: Common

Region: Found statewide but are more rare in the Mississippi lowlands

Diet: Herbivorous (leaves, flowers, grasses, wild herbs, crops, fruits, and vegetables)

SQUIRRELS STORE NUTS IN MULTIPLE LOCATIONS. THEY USE THEIR SPATIAL MEMORY AND OLFACTORY SENSES TO LOCATE THESE SECRET SNACKS, DIGGING THEM UP EVEN MONTHS LATER.

SQUIRRELS

Most Missourians see squirrels every day. We see them climbing trees, burying acorns, squished on the road, or preparing to wreak havoc in our neighbor's attic. Because squirrels are so common, we forget just how remarkable these creatures actually are. Like the beaver and the woodchuck, squirrels are rodents. Rodents are extremely successful at living in areas populated by humans, and squirrels are no exception. These guys are super rodents. If you take the time to truly watch squirrels, you may notice that they are extremely athletic. Aside from their talent for breaking into bird feeders, squirrels are quick runners, agile climbers, and incredible at leaping from limb to limb. They can jump up to 10 feet horizontally and six feet vertically! The majority of squirrels in Missouri are eastern gray squirrels or eastern fox squirrels. It's easy to spot a squirrel nest. Just look for a large cluster of leaves in the forking branches of a tree, though a hollow cavity is a preferred site for raising their young. A high-pitched, melodic whistling noise might alert you that a squirrel is home. In the fall, they will bury acorns, using visual and spatial clues throughout the season to remember where they buried their bounty. Any nuts that are forgotten can then grow into oak trees, ensuring a healthy crop for future generations of squirrels.

Scientific Name: *Sciurus carolinensis* ("gray squirrel") and *Sciurus niger* ("fox squirrel") (*Sciurus* translates to "shadow tail," and *carolinensis* refers to the Carolinas, while *niger* means "black.")

Order: Rodentia

Family: Sciuridae

Status: Common

Region: Found statewide, but the gray squirrel is more common in the Ozark and Mississippi Lowland regions, while the fox squirrel is more common in the northern and western plains.

Diet: Herbivorous (nuts, fruits and buds, and crops)

MOLES

Moles are synonymous with trouble. They're famous for creating annoying, lumpy tunnels through yards, and their name has been used to describe either a discolored patch of skin, a snitch, or a traitor. Not a great rep to build on! But look again. Moles are actually adorable. They have tiny, pink, pig-like snouts framed by fantastic whiskers and gummy, paddle-like front feet, shaped like stars. Plus, they put these cute features to good use. Moles live underground and are well adapted to their dark and (literally) dirty environment. The mole uses its big front feet to dig through its tunnels with a paddling motion. A single mole can dig a network of tunnels in just one night that spans more than 150 feet! These subterranean subdivisions can be used for finding food, nesting, or even storing caches of diet items. Moles have terrible eyesight. But excellent auditory and olfactory abilities make them well-trained for life underground. Though their bodies are quite rodent-like, moles are not rodents. Their closest cousins are actually animals like hedgehogs or shrews. Moles can eat more than half of their body weight in grubs, earthworms, beetles, centipedes, and spiders each day! Though they may be seen as a nuisance, in reality they help keep the soil healthy by aerating it, mixing in nutrients, and eating pest species. Plus, moles have been in North America for nearly 30 million years. Much longer than your backyard!

Scientific Name: *Scalopus aquaticus* ("water-dwelling blind rat") (Taxonomist Carl Linnaeus mistakenly thought moles were aquatic due to their webbed front feet.)

Order: Eulipotyphla

Family: Talpidae

Status: Common

Region: Statewide

Diet: Insectivorous (beetles, spiders, centipedes, pupae, and cutworms)

MOLES PREFER LOOSE, MOIST SOIL THAT IS EASY TO TUNNEL THROUGH. THIS MAKES LAWNS AND GARDENS PRIME DIGGING SPOTS.

SPRING PEEPERS

No, spring peepers are not bird-shaped marshmallows. They're actually a type of frog! In Missouri, the arrival of spring peepers heralds the end of winter and ushers in spring. Their calls sound like a combination of birds, crickets, and bells, and at the right time or near certain bodies of water, the sound is nearly deafening. This springtime symphony places the peeper into a genus called *Pseudacris*, or chorus frogs. These frogs typically hide under leaf litter during the day and become more active at dusk. Sometimes, they will "peep" out and call during the day when it is raining. So, if the arrival of spring peepers equals spring, where do these little frogs go in the winter? The answer: right here. They stay in Missouri, but they remain frozen. That's right; they make like Elsa the Ice Queen and allow themselves to freeze through the winter months (the cold doesn't bother them, anyway). Their hearts may stop, but a kind of antifreeze in their blood protects their tissues from damage. When temperatures warm up, the spring peeper thaws out, ready to sing, hop, and breed. It's actually the males who are doing most of the singing in their quest to find a mate. The female frog can lay around 1,000 eggs at one time, which are fertilized by the male. In a few days or weeks, depending on temperatures, the eggs will hatch into tadpoles who grow up into spring peeper frogs. Two years later the cycle starts all over again, their musical calls proclaiming the end of winter and making Missourians everywhere very hoppy.

Scientific Name: *Pseudacris crucifer* ("cross-bearing false locust")

Order: Anura

Family: Hylidae

Status: Common

Region: Found nearly statewide, except for the extreme northwestern corner of Missouri

Diet: Insectivorous (small insects and spiders on leaf litter)

SPRING PEEPERS ARE SMALL, ABOUT THE SIZE OF A PENNY.

Photo by Judy Gallagher/Wikimedia Commons
https://commons.wikimedia.org/w/index.php?curid=66901841

Photo by Christina Butler/Wikimedia Commons
https://commons.wikimedia.org/w/index.php?curid=95891578

HELLBENDERS SPEND THEIR DAYS TUCKED UNDER LARGE ROCKS.

HELLBENDERS

Hellbenders get their name because they look, well, sort of peculiar. The word "hellbender" was inspired by the belief that these salamanders look like they might have wandered out of Hades's realm and are "hell-bent" on returning. Not so! Hellbenders have no need for fire and brimstone. Instead, all they desire is a stream full of clean, spring-fed, running water. They walk on the bottom of streambeds, hunting crayfish at night and minding their own business. When breeding season comes around, the males will fertilize a clutch of 200 to 500 eggs through a process called external fertilization. Then these dedicated dads will defend their developing offspring for 45 to 60 days until they hatch. Hellbenders are one of the largest species of salamander in the world. They can grow to two feet in length and live for 20-plus years. Missouri is the only state that is home to both subspecies of hellbender—the eastern hellbender and the Ozark hellbender. Unfortunately, both species of hellbender are listed as endangered species, due to disease, habitat loss, and water quality in the streams where they make their homes. Fortunately, scientists from the Missouri Department of Conservation and the Saint Louis Zoo are on the case. To date, they have released more than 10,000 hellbenders back into the wild, buying the species time while we try to solve the problems causing their decline.

Scientific Name: *Cryptobranchus alleganiensis bishopi* ("Ozark hellbender") and *Cryptobranchus alleganiensis* ("eastern hellbender") (The Ozark hellbender's scientific name honors American herpetologist Sherman C. Bishop, while *Cryptobranchus* translates to "hidden gill" and *alleganiensis* means "from the Allegheny River system.")

Order: Urodela

Family: Cryptobranchidae

Status: Both species are endangered.

Region: The Ozark hellbender is restricted to southern Missouri and northern Arkansas. Eastern hellbenders occur in spring-fed rivers in the northern Ozark highlands of Missouri.

Diet: Carnivorous (fish, crayfish, or small invertebrates)

Photo by Quartl/Wikimedia Commons
https://commons.wikimedia.org/wiki/File:Agkistrodon_contortrix_qtl1.jpg

COPPERHEADS GROW TO AN AVERAGE OF TWO TO THREE FEET LONG.

COPPERHEADS

Did you know that there are five species of venomous snakes here in Missouri? They are the cottonmouth, the western pygmy rattlesnake, the massasauga rattlesnake, the timber rattlesnake, and the copperhead—with the copperhead being the most common and well-known. Copperheads are easy to recognize with their distinctive, coppery brown scales. Sometimes other snakes like the juvenile eastern rat snake, the corn snake, or the northern water snake can be mistaken for copperheads because of their similar appearance. But, like many other venomous snakes, copperheads have vertical, diamond-shaped—rather than round—pupils. Don't get too close, though! If you're not sure what kind of snake you are seeing, give it some space. Venomous snakes are not aggressive if left undisturbed. If you leave them alone, they will leave you alone too. Though you'll often hear of copperheads being referred to as "poisonous snakes," such a thing actually does not exist! Poison has to be ingested (for example, if you eat a poison dart frog, you will get sick), while venom is injected, in this case through the snake's fangs. So, copperheads are technically a venomous, not poisonous, snake species. They are semi-social snakes, meaning while they typically hunt alone, they often hibernate with other snakes and return to the same dens every winter. Copperheads are also ovoviviparous—meaning that the female's eggs incubate inside of her, and then she gives birth to live young with shockingly green tails that act as lures to help the young snakes hunt. Baby snakes with neon scales may sound cute, but watch out! They are born with fangs and venom just as potent as mom's.

Scientific Name: *Agkistrodon contortrix* ("hook-toothed" and "twisted")

Order: Squamata

Family: Viperidae

Status: Common

Region: Statewide

Diet: Carnivorous (small mammals, reptiles, amphibians, small birds, and insects)

Photo by Alan Rockefeller/Wikimedia Commons https://commons.wikimedia.org/wiki/File:Agkistrodon_contortrix_242284249.jpg

COTTONMOUTHS

The cottonmouth, also known as the water moccasin, is one of Missouri's five venomous snake species. The cottonmouth gets its name from the white outline of its mouth. When the snake is alarmed, it will open its mouth in a defensive posture, showing off its "cotton." Common, nonvenomous water snakes are often mistaken for cottonmouths. Many people are afraid of snakes and will kill them, especially if they are venomous. Have you ever been on a float trip and had a snake drop into your canoe? These are usually nonvenomous water snakes, not cottonmouths. Cottonmouths prefer to hang out on the ground near waterways, and they rarely climb trees. Plus, they live only south of the Missouri River, so you will not see them in the northern part of the state. Cottonmouths also have a habit of vibrating their tails when feeling threatened. Water snakes don't do this. It's important to know how to identify animal species, whether by their appearance or by their behavior, when you are exploring the wild. These skills can save snake lives! And we want plenty of healthy snakes—even venomous ones—in our ecosystem. Snakes like cottonmouths keep rodent populations under control. Sometimes cottonmouths will even help us by cleaning up roadkill! We all need to work to protect these special snakes. In fact, cottonmouths are protected by Missouri's Wildlife Code. It is actually against the law to kill, harm, or harass them. Now that's what I call ssssssmart!

Scientific Name: *Agkistrodon piscivorus* ("hook-toothed fish eater")

Order: Squamata

Family: Viperidae

Status: Common in the southeastern corner of Missouri

Region: Not found north of the Missouri River

Diet: Carnivorous (fish, small mammals, reptiles, amphibians, small birds, and insects)

COTTONMOUTHS CAN WANDER AWAY FROM WATER BUT PREFER TO STAY NEAR WETLANDS.

Courtesy of CDC

Photo by Peter Paplanus/Wikimedia Commons
https://commons.wikimedia.org/wiki/File:Timber_Rattlesnake_(Crotalus_horridus)_(31140366037).jpg

IN THE WINTER, TIMBER RATTLESNAKES DEN COMMUNALLY IN ROCK CREVICES OR LEDGES.

RATTLESNAKES

Chicachicachicachica! What is that infamous sound? Why, a rattlesnake, of course! Rattlesnakes have long been the stuff of legend. Whether they are setting the scene in a western or playing a part in Native American mythology, rattlesnakes have always held their place in our collective imaginations. We are so lucky to have three species of rattlesnake living in Missouri: the timber rattlesnake, the western pygmy rattlesnake, and the massasauga rattlesnake. In evolutionary terms, rattlesnakes are advanced. They have hollow fangs for injecting venom (not poison, remember?) and heat-detecting facial "pits" that help them to sense their warm-blooded prey. But their rattles are what really make them special. The rattles help to warn off other animals that might hurt them, saving the snake the energy and venom needed to attack. Even though the rattling might sound scary, these snakes are actually doing us a favor, saying loud and clear, "Get back!" before it's too late. Western pygmy rattlesnakes live in southern Missouri and are elusive, making them rare to see in the wild. The massasauga rattlesnake lives in northern Missouri and is even harder to find. But the timber rattlesnake is found throughout the state and is Missouri's largest venomous snake. Don't let that, ahem, rattle you. Most Missourians don't see these reptiles very often because even big, venomous snakes like the timber rattlesnake can be quite shy. If you do see a snake, it likely will be basking in the sun on a nice day. Snakes like rattlesnakes are ectothermic—meaning their body temperature is regulated by external sources. When they need to warm up they may seek out sun, and if they need to chill out they might head for the shade. Pretty cool!

Scientific Name: *Crotalus horridus* (timber rattlesnake; "horrible rattle"), *Sistrurus miliarius streckeri* (western pygmy rattlesnake; "millet-like rattlesnake"), and *Sistrurus catenatus* (massasauga rattlesnake; "chain-tailed")

Order: Squamata

Family: Viperidae

Status: Timber rattlesnake numbers are declining. Western pygmy rattlesnakes are quite rare to see in Missouri. The massasauga rattlesnake is listed as endangered in Missouri due to habitat loss and reduced population.

Region: Timber rattlesnakes were formerly found statewide but are now eliminated from multiple counties. Western pygmy rattlesnakes are found in the southern border of Missouri and Arkansas and in the Ozarks. Massasauga rattlesnakes are found in isolated populations in north-central counties and in the northwestern corner of the state.

Diet: Carnivorous (fish, small mammals, reptiles, amphibians, small birds, and insects)

SNAPPING TURTLES

Oh, snap! What is the largest group of turtle species in Missouri? It's the snapping turtles! We have two types of snapping turtles in Missouri—the alligator snapping turtle and the eastern snapping turtle. The eastern, or common, snapping turtle is much more common in our state. The alligator snappers can sometimes be seen farther south, closer to the Arkansas border. Both species boast a formidable bite. Snapping turtles can crush, or even bite through, bone or metal. It's important to leave these turtles be when encountered in the wild. They've been known to occasionally bite off fingers! Snapping turtles usually make use of their bite force to munch on prey items like insects, crayfish, fish, or even snakes, birds, or small mammals. The alligator snapping turtle has a nifty adaptation for hunting. Its tongue resembles an earthworm. If it sits still enough with its mouth open underwater, this tempting tongue might lure an unsuspecting fish into the snapper's mighty maw. Turtles like common and alligator snappers also have a sort of silly adaptation. They can breathe out of their butts! The fancier way to describe this ability is cloacal respiration. Turtles can use this skill when hibernating in the winter, or while diving. Basically, turtles are able to use their all-purpose hole—the cloaca—to diffuse oxygen from water into their bloodstream. Now that is a talented tush!

Scientific Name: *Chelydra serpentina* (common snapping turtle; translates to "tortoise and snake," a reference to the turtle's long tail) and *Macrochelys temminckii* (alligator snapping turtle; *Macrochelys* means a "large turtle," and *temminckii* is in honor of Dutch zoologist Coenraad Jacob Temminck)

Order: Testudines

Family: Chelydridae

Status: Eastern snapping turtles are common throughout the state. Alligator snapping turtles are a species of conservation concern in Missouri.

Region: South of the Missouri River

Diet: Omnivorous (insects, crayfish, fish, snails, worms, amphibians, snakes, small turtles, small mammals, birds, aquatic vegetation, and carrion; alligator snapping turtles will also eat nuts and fruits or mussels)

SNAPPING TURTLES LIKE TO BURY THEMSELVES IN MUD WITH ONLY THEIR EYES AND NOSE EXPOSED.

BOX TURTLES HAVE A SHARP BEAK TO TEAR FOOD ITEMS INTO SMALLER PIECES.

BOX TURTLES

Many Missourians have seen a box turtle. They are commonly spotted crunching through leaves in the woods, crossing the road, or even exploring our backyards. But what many people don't realize is just how special these reptiles really are. The box turtle is the only species of turtle that can completely "close up" its shell. Despite what's seen in cartoons, turtles cannot exit their shells—or carapace, if we're being scientific. Their spine runs along their length. Box turtles have a special hinge along the bottom part of their shell called the plastron. The plastron allows them to close or "box up" for protection. Missouri is home to 17 species of turtles, including two species of box turtle: the ornate box turtle and the three-toed box turtle. The three-toed box turtle is Missouri's state reptile! Ornate box turtles have "fancier" shells with orange-and-yellow markings. Three-toed box turtles typically sport the "classic" turtle coloration of greenish brown. These two species can reproduce together though, hatching hybrids. Regardless of their carapace coloring, box turtles are long-lived, with lifespans up to 50 years! There's a lot to learn about box turtles. The Forest Park Living Lab tracks box turtles in St. Louis's Forest Park using radio telemetry. These scientists collect important data about turtle health and movement patterns. You too might have the chance to see a box turtle crossing the road during their breeding season in the summer. Often, these turtles are males in search of a mate. If it is safe to do so, drivers can pull over to assist turtles in their crossing. But make sure that you set them on the other side pointing in the same direction they were going. A turtle on a mission will continue on its set path, regardless of any hazards in its way.

Scientific Name: *Terrapene ornata ornata* ("ornate" or "fancy turtle") and *Terrapene carolina triunguis* ("three-toed turtle from the Carolinas")

Order: Testudines

Family: Emydidae

Status: Ornate box turtles are a species of concern due to declining populations, habitat destruction, and the pet trade. Three-toed box turtles can be abundant but are generally declining statewide, as well.

Region: Ornate box turtles are found statewide, except for the southeastern corner of the state. Three-toed box turtles are found statewide, except for the extreme northern and northwestern parts of the state.

Diet: Omnivorous (worms, insects, plant matter, fungi, grasses, and snails)

TIGER SALAMANDERS

There are tigers in Missouri! And no, I don't just mean Truman at Mizzou. Missouri is home to tiger salamanders, to be precise. And they are just as cool as their namesake kin. Missouri is home to 50 species and subspecies of salamander, with tiger salamanders found throughout the state. The word salamander translates from the Greek for "fire animal." That's because these elusive amphibians often hide under logs and will scurry out when their shelters are tossed on a fire. This made some people believe that salamanders actually came from fire. Spoiler alert: They don't. Though many might call them lizards, salamanders are actually amphibians, meaning that like frogs and toads, they breathe through their skin. This is what nerdy scientists refer to as cutaneous respiration. Tiger salamanders get their name from their unique coloration. They are typically black or dark brown with yellow splotches (Mizzou-rah!). They are part of a family of amphibians called mole salamanders, aptly named because they spend most of their life in burrows underground. Despite the myth that they are forged from fire, salamanders actually need fishless ponds to survive. Here, the females lay clumps of up to 1,000 eggs in early spring. Like other amphibians, their young are born entirely aquatic with gills to breathe underwater.

Scientific Name: *Ambystoma tigrinum* ("blunt mouth" and "like a tiger")

Order: Urodela

Family: Ambystomatidae

Status: A species of concern in Missouri with declining population

Region: Presumed statewide but more common in the northern half of the state

Diet: Carnivorous (invertebrates, small mice, frogs or snakes, worms, spiders, slugs, snails, and even other salamanders)

THE BREEDING SEASON FOR TIGER SALAMANDERS IS OFTEN AFTER HEAVY RAINS IN THE LATE WINTER TO EARLY SPRING.

EASTERN BLUEBIRDS WEIGH ABOUT AN OUNCE AND MEASURE JUST SIX TO EIGHT INCHES IN LENGTH, WITH A WINGSPAN OF 10 TO 13 INCHES.

EASTERN BLUEBIRDS

Bluebirds are synonymous with happiness. And who wouldn't be happy when spotting a bluebird? These little birds are beautiful, with their bright blue backs and rust-colored chests. Henry David Thoreau once wrote that "[the bluebird] carries the sky on its back." Their song is cheery, and they bring an air of springtime whimsy wherever they flit or fly. Aren't we lucky to have such a delightful animal as our state bird? The eastern bluebird was declared the state bird of Missouri in 1927. They are common here and remain so because of civilian efforts to build "bluebird boxes." Their nesting season is from late February through early September, and these special boxes encourage them to nest in the area. Bluebirds are cavity nesters, meaning they like to make their homes inside of trees. Because humans like to remove dead trees, there are often not enough cavities available. This leaves chicks vulnerable to dangerous predators. Bluebird boxes give these bright little birds a good start, allowing them to make nests in a safe space. You can find instructions for building a bluebird box on the National Audubon Society's website. Bluebirds appreciate the help because they are very busy parents, often raising two or even three broods each summer. Building a nesting box in your backyard gives you a front-row seat to watch a bluebird family grow!

Scientific Name: *Sialia sialis* ("a type of bird")

Order: Passeriformes

Family: Turdidae

Status: Common statewide in the summer, uncommon in the south, and rare in the north in the winter

Region: Statewide in summer, more common in the south in winter

Diet: Omnivorous (fruits and insects)

GREAT HORNED OWLS

Who . . . whooooo is that, flying silently through the night? It could be a great horned owl! Missouri is home to eight species of owl, with the great horned being the largest. The great horned owl is the classic "hoot owl," meaning that its call really does sound like it is saying "Hoo! Hoo!" Great horned owls are sometimes known as the "wolves of the sky" because they are apex predators. Apex predators are hunters at the very top of the food chain. Part of their prowess comes from their ability to fly silently. Their wing feathers have serrated edges and soft fringe that muffles the sound of air passing over them. This enables owls to sneak up on their prey. Great horned owls can also be identified by their ear tufts (not actual ears, just feathers), which give them the name "horned." Those tufts aren't real ears, but great horned owls do have incredible hearing. They can hear a single mouse scurrying around under a foot of snow! Like other owls, they are nocturnal hunters with an expansive menu. Great horned owls usually dine on small rodents and mammals like mice, rabbits, and squirrels but have been observed attacking animals as large as great blue herons, other owls, or even turkeys. Because they have a very poor sense of smell, they are one of the few animals who can also eat skunks. How about that for a takeout odor!

Scientific Name: *Bubo virginianus* (first documented in the Virginia colonies by European naturalists; *Bubo* means "horned owl")

Order: Strigiformes

Family: Strigidae

Status: Common

Region: Statewide

Diet: Carnivorous (mice, insects, other birds, snakes, rabbits, and skunks)

GREAT HORNED OWLS ARE HIGHLY ADAPTABLE AND CAN LIVE IN FORESTS, RIVER VALLEYS, AND EVEN URBAN PARKS.

SNOWY EGRETS BUILD PLATFORMS OF STICKS IN TREES OR SHRUBS OVER WATER.

SNOWY EGRETS

Birds are here, there, and everywhere! That's because they migrate. Some species can be found here in Missouri and also be seen wintering on tropical shores. One such bird is the snowy egret, named for its snow-white plumage. The snowy egret flaunts a long, elegant neck and decorative head feathers. These feathers once spelled trouble for the egret. Have you ever seen an illustration or a movie depicting the Victorian era? Often, women in these scenes are wearing hats adorned with fantastical feathers. These feathers came from birds like snowy egrets. In fact, the demand for Victorian hat feathers almost drove this beautiful bird to extinction. Happily, in 1913, the United States Congress passed the Weeks–McLean Law, also known as the Migratory Bird Act. This law made hunting protected birds for their feathers illegal. Legislation outlawed the interstate transport of birds, seriously damaging the trade of plumes for decorative hats. Weeks–McLean, followed by the Migratory Bird Treaty Act in 1918, essentially saved the snowy egret from a sad fate. More than 100 years later, conservationists in Missouri are still working to help birds like egrets. Their wetland habitat homes are at risk of being destroyed. Many migratory birds, like snowy egrets, need these swamps to survive. Wetlands and swamps are important ecosystems that function as sponges to protect our state from major flooding. They also serve as both a nursery and a restaurant for all of our high-flying and migrating friends. Our swamps deserve to be celebrated, along with the snowy egrets that call them home.

Scientific Name: *Egretta thula* (*Egretta* means "heron," and *thula* comes, by mistake, from the Araucano term for "black-necked swan," given to the egret on accident by Chilean naturalist Juan Ignacio Molina.)

Order: Pelecaniformes

Family: Ardeidae

Status: Endangered in the state of Missouri due to habitat destruction and human disturbances

Region: Southeastern corner of the state along the Mississippi River

Diet: Carnivorous (worms, fish, small rodents, amphibians, reptiles, and crayfish)

TURKEY VULTURES

Who has a naked head, poops on its feet to cool off, and vomits on its enemies? That's right, the turkey vulture! Sounds appealing, right? Vultures across the world get a bad rap. They are seen as omens of death in many cultures because they eat dead things and tend to congregate when death is nigh. But let's imagine for a moment a world without vultures. There would be a lot more dead things lying around, which means more smell, more mess, and more disease. In fact, vultures are doing all of us a big favor by acting as nature's consummate cleanup crew. Those features that seem a bit nasty are simply helpful adaptations for performing their job. The naked head allows the vulture to stick its beak inside of body cavities without getting its feathers too messy. And considering what a vulture eats, vomiting on its enemies is a pretty ingenious defense strategy. Turkey vultures can often be seen with wings outstretched, riding thermals in the sky. They're a common sight. But did you know that turkey vultures have one of the best senses of smell of any animal that has ever lived? That's right . . . ever! They can smell dead things from miles away, even while flying. Turkey vultures don't deserve disgust; instead they deserve respect. They are essential workers within the ecosystem of our state.

Scientific Name: *Cathartes aura* ("golden purifier")

Order: Accipitriformes

Family: Cathartidae

Status: Common migrant and summer resident

Region: Found statewide, though less common in the southeastern part of Missouri. In parts of southern Missouri they are becoming more common in the winter, as well.

Diet: Carnivorous (carrion)

TURKEY VULTURES ARE NAMED FOR THEIR RESEMBLANCE TO WILD TURKEYS.

MULES

This is a book about amazing Missouri animals, so naturally it must include the state animal of Missouri. Here's a hint; it's big with long ears, and it rhymes with cool. You got it. The animal that represents the state of Missouri is . . . the mule! The mule became the official state animal in 1995. Mules are a hybrid species. They are the offspring of a female horse and a male donkey, so they have characteristics of both, though they cannot reproduce. Like many Missourians, mules are known for being hardy, smart, and hardworking. They have a long history in our state. They pulled the pioneer wagons rolling westward through our "Gateway to the West" and plowed the farm fields that helped early settlers grow food. They moved troops and supplies during both world wars and became one of Missouri's breeding exports. The University of Missouri in Columbia boasts not only one of the best veterinary schools in the country but also its own mule team! The mules are cared for by veterinary students and appear at various parades and events. Newly minted doctors of veterinary medicine even get to have their graduation photos taken with the beloved mules. With their size, strength, and intelligence, these animals bring together the best of both horses and donkeys. Now, I'd say that makes the Missouri mule pretty darn cool.

Scientific Name: *Equus mulus* ("horse mule")

Order: Perissodactyla

Family: Equidae

Status: Domesticated

Diet: Herbivorous (hay, grain, grass, and produce)

MULES CAN RESEMBLE EITHER PARENT AND ARE KNOWN FOR THEIR INTELLIGENCE AND SURE-FOOTEDNESS.

Courtesy of Missouri State Archives

JIM THE WONDER DOG

Missouri is home to lots of amazing species, and some incredible individual animals too. Take, for example, the legendary story of Jim the Wonder Dog. Jim was a Llewellin setter who lived in Marshall, Missouri, in the late 1920s and throughout the 1930s. Jim's owner, Sam VanArsdale, trained him to hunt quail. As it turned out, Jim was an incredible hunting companion. He could find quail better than any of Sam's other dogs. One day, Sam asked Jim to "go rest for a bit under the hickory tree." Jim actually went and lay beneath a hickory! Sam tried the same command with a walnut, a cedar, a stump, and even a tin can, and Jim performed each of these tasks to a tee. From that day forward, Jim continued to prove himself to be a true wonder dog. He could differentiate individuals by their occupation or where they were from. He could identify cars by make and model. He perfectly executed commands in foreign languages, shorthand, and Morse code. He even performed his feats in front of the Missouri legislature and at the Missouri State Fair! Nobody knows how Jim accomplished so much. Was it a canine version of the "Clever Hans Effect," meaning that Jim was just really good at reading unconscious human cues? Was VanArsdale somehow fooling his adoring crowds? Or was Jim the Wonder Dog truly a miracle mutt? We may never know, but we can still appreciate and celebrate one of Missouri's most prominent pups. In Marshall, you can visit a Jim the Wonder Dog Museum and Garden that features a sculpture of Jim.

Scientific Name: *Canis lupus familiaris* ("dog wolf of the household")

Order: Carnivora

Family: Canidae

Breed: Llewellin setter

Years: 1925–1937

Diet: Omnivorous (dog chow)

Above photo courtesy of Missouri State Archives and Friends of Jim the Wonder Dog

IN 2017 THE MISSOURI GENERAL ASSEMBLY DESIGNATED JIM THE OFFICIAL "MISSOURI STATE WONDER DOG." AND WHY WOULDN'T THEY? AMONG OTHER FEATS, HE CORRECTLY PREDICETED THE WINNER OF SEVEN KENTUCKY DERBIES!

LILY THE SEARCH AND RESCUE DOG

On May 22, 2011, a category F5 tornado hit Joplin, Missouri. It was the deadliest storm in Missouri history, and one of the deadliest tornadoes to ever hit the US. When bad things happen in our communities, there are always helpers that rise to the occasion. Helpers come in all shapes and sizes. Sometimes, they can even be dogs! Lily was a trained search and rescue dog who grew up in Joplin. As a Weimaraner, Lily was born with an incredible sense of smell. After the Joplin tornado, Lily and her owner, Tara Prosser, put that good nose to use. They investigated the wreckage, looking for survivors or people who were hurt. To train a dog to work under such intense conditions requires dedication and skill. During training exercises, Prosser taught Lily to identify a single baby tooth in the middle of an open field. Lily also practiced her skills by playing hide-and-seek with Prosser's kids. All of this training paid off. When her community needed her, Lily was ready. But a search and rescue dog's job is never easy. After the tornado, Lily got glass in her paws. She worked through intense thunderstorms. And she had to help Prosser conquer her fear of heights while they searched the roof of the local hospital. But through her bravery, this determined duo was able to stand by their motto to live right, train hard, and fight the good fight, helping their community along the way.

Scientific Name: *Canis lupus familiaris* ("dog wolf of the household")

Order: Carnivora

Family: Canidae

Breed: Weimaraner

Years: 2007–2017

Diet: Omnivorous (dog chow)

LILY WAS FEATURED IN A CHILDREN'S BOOK TITLED *LILY: A TRUE STORY OF COURAGE AND THE JOPLIN TORNADO.*

Photos by Tara Prosser

Photo by Kelly Brownfield

MAVERICK WORKS WITH THE USO MISSOURI AS A THERAPY DOG.

MAVERICK THE GREAT DANE

Maverick the Great Dane is a true gentle giant. At 150 pounds, this big, gray dog may look intimidating. But in reality, he's a sweet-natured soul who found his purpose as a steadfast companion to our troops and their families on military bases. Maverick lives with his handler, Kelly Brownfield, at Fort Leonard Wood in south central Missouri. There, Maverick serves as a therapy dog. He helps soldiers who are having a difficult time. Because he is so big, Maverick is a quiet, steady presence for these women and men. He offers comfort and unconditional love in their times of need. He also visits schools where many of the students have parents in the military. The kids can read to him, pet him, or just snuggle up with him. Just as Maverick is able to lend a "helping paw" to the soldiers at Fort Leonard Wood, he has also guided their children through their own challenges. In 2023, Maverick won the award for both American Humane Hero Dog of the Year (overall in all categories) and American Humane Therapy Dog of the Year for his work. Further cementing his hero status, both Maverick and Brownfield are cancer survivors. Maverick was able to bring comfort to Brownfield through her cancer journey, helping them both to get to the other side. Living up to his breed's reputation, Maverick certainly puts the "great" in Great Dane!

Scientific Name: *Canis lupus familiaris* ("dog wolf of the household")

Order: Carnivora

Family: Canidae

Breed: Great Dane

Born: 2017

Diet: Omnivorous (dog chow)

Photo by Kelly Brownfield

BOBCATS HAVE INTERESTING NAMES. A FEMALE BOBCAT IS CALLED A "QUEEN" AND A MALE BOBCAT IS CALLED A "TOM."

BOBCATS

Bobcats are one of the most exciting species to spot in Missouri! They used to be found primarily in the bootheel, but they now live in a variety of environments throughout the state. A bobcat is, as its name states, a member of the felid family, meaning . . . it's a cat. Though they may be cute, with their pointed ears and speckled coats, these animals are no house kitties. Bobcats, like their fellow cat cousins, are obligate carnivores, so they eat only meat. Though they mostly hunt small mammals like rabbits, mice, rats, and squirrels, they have occasionally been known to take down prey as large as deer. They can even leap 12 feet vertically into the air! Though they are not huge animals, weighing in at only 11 to 30 pounds, they are fast. Bobcats can run up to 30 miles per hour! For perspective, Usain Bolt, the fastest human in the world, clocks in at 27 miles per hour at top speed. You can't outrun a bobcat, no matter how fancy your sneakers. These crepuscular carnivores feature heavily in Indigenous folklore, their legendary status cemented by their eerie "scream." This mating call can sound very human. Those lucky enough to hear it describe it as similar to a woman screeching or a baby crying. Though they may be fierce, these animals are still quite cute. Baby bobcats are adorably known as bobkittens.

Scientific Name: *Lynx rufus* ("red lynx")

Order: Carnivora

Family: Felidae

Status: Currently stable

Region: Statewide. Bobcats used to be found mostly in the Ozarks and bootheel, but they have expanded westward and northward.

Diet: Carnivorous (deer, small mammals, and birds)

WHITE-TAILED DEER

Whether you've seen them grazing in a roadside field, leaping through the woods, or sprinting across a road, or you've spied their heart-shaped tracks imprinted in the mud, white-tailed deer are all around us. Deer are widespread in Missouri, and they play a central role in our ecosystem. Deer are prey animals for our apex predators like bobcats and coyotes. They also help to maintain our forests. When they nip off the buds from branches, they encourage growth on their favorite foraging plants. But too many deer can be a problem. They can overeat the forests so that it is harder for the vegetation to regrow. They can also spread disease and cause conflict on motorways. Most deer sightings happen at dawn and dusk. Only male white-tailed deer—called bucks—grow antlers. These antlers aren't just for show; they come in handy when competing for females, or does. Two males might use their antlers to spar with one another in competition for a mate. The females will give birth to between one and three fawns in the springtime. Twins are the most common! When they are born they have white, speckled coats that help them to hide in the forest thicket. As the deer grows older, these spots will eventually fade away. Now that is a deer-lightful way to stay camouflaged!

WHITE-TAILED DEER ARE THE MOST COMMON LARGE MAMMAL IN MISSOURI.

Scientific Name: *Odocoileus virginianus* ("hollow-toothed of Virginia")

Order: Artiodactyla

Family: Cervidae

Status: Common

Region: Statewide

Diet: Herbivorous (grasses, leaves, nuts, berries, fruits, and flowers)

NORTH AMERICAN RIVER OTTERS

North American river otters are some of the cutest, smartest, most adaptable animals in Missouri. So how can anyone see them as a nuisance? Well, otters are carnivorous, and humans around the world sometimes struggle with living alongside meat eaters. Centuries of fur trapping and habitat destruction left only about 35 to 70 otters in Missouri by 1980. In 1982, a group of otters was brought to Missouri from Louisiana. Over the next 11 years, 845 otters were released, and they thrived in their new habitat. Their population eventually grew to more than 15,000 otters! Their competition with humans centered around fish. Otters eat a lot of fish. They are incredibly adept at catching their meals. So good, in fact, that fishers will often find themselves frustrated by the depletion of fish in common lakes and ponds. In 1996, the Missouri Department of Conservation started a trapping program that reduced the number of otters. Today otters and anglers in Missouri are able to share the land and the fish, working to strike the right balance for our natural resources. The plus side? Plenty of fish for the anglers and more opportunities to spot these delightful mustelids sliding down Missouri's muddy riverbanks.

Scientific Name: *Lontra canadensis* ("otter from Canada")

Order: Carnivora

Family: Mustelidae

Status: Common

Region: Statewide

Diet: Carnivorous (fish, crayfish, mussels, frogs, turtles, birds, and small mammals)

NORTH AMERICAN RIVER OTTERS TYPICALLY DIVE UNDERWATER FOR THREE TO FOUR MINUTES BUT CAN HOLD THEIR BREATH FOR UP TO EIGHT MINUTES!

SPINY SOFTSHELL TURTLES

Which animal has a flat back like a pancake, webbed feet like a duck, and a nose like a pig? The spiny softshell turtle! Seventeen species of turtle live in Missouri, but the spiny softshell is arguably one of the strangest and cutest. Spiny softshell turtles are an aquatic species, meaning that they spend the majority of their time in the water. Their little pig noses act like snorkels and can poke above the surface so that the turtle can take a breath. Their flat backs make it easy for them to slide under mud or sand to hide, hunt, or hibernate. We've already learned about box turtles and snapping turtles. Those species have a hard carapace, which is slightly domed. Softshell turtles are different. Their shells are soft and rubbery and lined with tiny spines. Hence the name, spiny softshell. Like the snapping turtle, they are one of the biggest freshwater turtles in Missouri. The females are actually larger than the males, so technically it's the girls who get to take home the turtle size prize! Reptiles are commonly long lived, and softshell turtles are no exception. Spiny softshell turtles can live for up to 50 years.

Scientific Name: *Apalone spinifera* ("soft and thorn/spine-bearing")

Order: Testudines

Family: Trionychidae

Status: Common

Region: Statewide

Diet: Primarily carnivorous (crayfish, insects, worms, snails, mussels, fish, tadpoles, and sometimes aquatic plants)

SPINY SOFTSHELL TURTLES ARE FAST ON LAND AND WATER AND CAN DART QUICKLY TO ESCAPE PREDATORS.

THE FEMALES NEST IN TALL GRASSES AND LAY ANYWHERE FROM SEVEN TO 17 EGGS PER CLUTCH.

GREATER PRAIRIE CHICKENS

Many of the animals in this book, like white-tailed deer and squirrels, are common in Missouri. But a few species are endangered. Meet the greater prairie chicken! This bird is not a chicken at all but rather a species of grouse. Missouri is a gateway state, a bridge between the forests of the East and the prairies of the West. In the western part of the state, prairies are part of the landscape, blending into Kansas and Oklahoma. These prairies are the natural habitat for the greater prairie chicken. Unfortunately, in the 21st century, true prairie is hard to find. This loss of habitat creates a problem for the greater prairie chicken. Once a prized game bird, there are now fewer than 100 individuals in our state. We want to help the greater prairie chicken and increase their population! One reason? Well, their rather colorful mating rituals are a sight to behold. To vie for the attention of a female, the male greater prairie chicken inflates his vibrant orange throat sac and dances around with his head feathers pointed up like horns. Romantic, right? But it's not just their flair for the eccentric that makes them important. Healthy populations of greater prairie chickens are indicative of healthy grassland ecosystems. Healthy grassland prairies support an innumerable number of native species. And each one is an important resident in our state.

Scientific Name: *Tympanuchus cupido* ("drum bearer of desire")

Order: Galliformes

Family: Phasianidae

Status: Endangered

Region: Native prairie and grasslands in the Osage Plains and Glaciated Plains

Diet: Omnivorous (insects, seeds, greens, and grains)

BURYING BEETLES

Endangered species come in all shapes and sizes. Some even have six legs! Missouri was once home to a rare and beautiful insect, the American burying beetle. American burying beetles might look handsome, with their vibrant red-and-black coloring, but their habits are a tad gross. These guys have the somewhat horrifying habit of embalming carrion with naturally secreted fluids. Typically, a male and female work together to bury a dead animal. It can be a mammal, reptile, or bird—their tastes are not very particular! The couple will lay their eggs next to these wretched remains, the eggs hatch into grubs, and voila! The corpse is transformed into an all-you-can-eat buffet. Mom and Dad work together to care for their young by regurgitating some of this meat into their larvae's mouths. Yum! The larvae eventually pupate and emerge aboveground as full-fledged adults a few months later. And the cycle begins again! Unfortunately, burying beetles have disappeared from around 90 percent of their historic range, including in Missouri. The Saint Louis Zoo is working to reintroduce zoo-bred beetles back into their native habitats, as well as surveying existing populations. Scientists don't really know what caused burying beetle populations to drop so dramatically, but it likely has to do with habitat destruction and fragmentation of our native prairies. The work continues to increase their numbers because as gross as their behavior may seem, they serve an important role in helping to keep our prairie ecosystems healthy and clean.

Scientific Name: *Nicrophorus americanus* ("American death carrier")

Order: Coleoptera

Family: Silphidae

Status: Endangered

Region: Formerly statewide, now only in limited areas with reintroduced populations

Diet: Carnivorous (other insects and carrion)

WHEN BURYING BEETLES FEED THEIR LARVAE, THEY CALL THEM OVER BY MAKING SQUEAKING SOUNDS WITH THEIR WINGS.

MISSOURI FOX TROTTERS

Missouri has a lot of state symbols. There's an official insect, tree, flower, instrument, song, amphibian, fossil, and fish, to name a few. Missouri even has its own official state horse: the Missouri fox trotter! Missouri fox trotters have a long history here. They originated in the Ozark hills in the early 1800s, their bloodlines going back to the first settlers that came to the land from neighboring states like Kentucky, Illinois, Tennessee, and Arkansas. Though many breeds of horses are distinguished by the color of their coat or the size and texture of their bodies or manes, fox trotters are different. They are notable for the differences in their gait, or the way that they move. A fox trot is a short, broken, slow trotting movement in which the hind foot of the horse hits the ground just before the diagonally opposite forefoot. Missouri fox trotters were officially designated as a breed in 1948. The town of Ava, Missouri, is the home of the Missouri Fox Trotting Horse Breed Association and hosts an annual show and celebration of these elegant horses. Every first full week of September, during the show, it's officially Missouri Fox Trotter Week in our state.

Scientific Name: *Equus ferus caballus* ("a working horse descended from a wild ancestor")

Order: Perissodactyla

Family: Equidae

Status: Domesticated

Diet: Herbivorous (grass, grain, and hay)

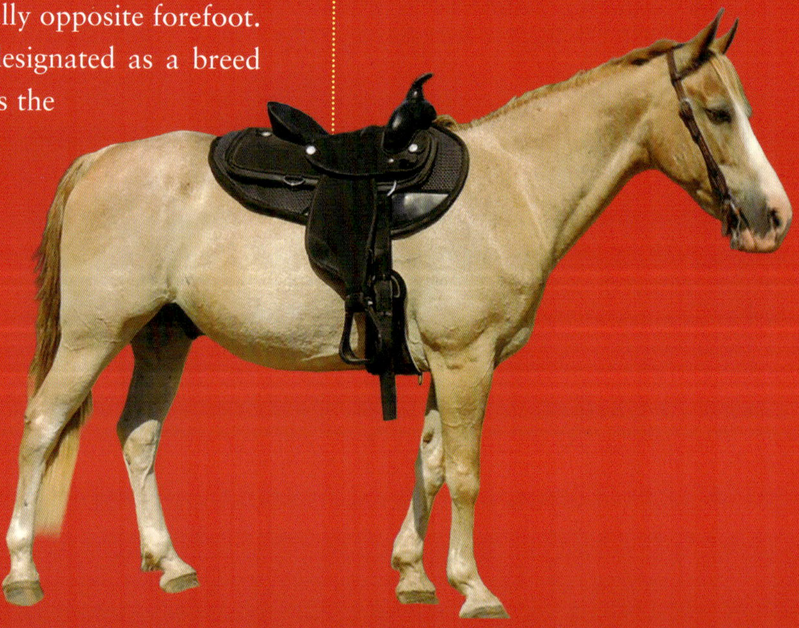

Photo by Gaitedhorse/Wikimedia Commons https://commons.wikimedia.org/w/index.php?curid=62353523

Photo by Kayla Oakes/Wikimedia Commons
https://commons.wikimedia.org/w/index.php?curid=12602351

MISSOURI FOX TROTTERS ARE EXPORTED NATIONALLY AND INTERNATIONALLY AS A POPULAR TRAIL AND PLEASURE HORSE.

Courtesy of Missouri State Archives

OLD DRUM THE DOG

One of the harsh realities of loving a dog is encountering the grief that comes when the dog passes away. The untimely death of Old Drum, a beloved hound dog, was the centerpiece of a famous court case that made its way to the Supreme Court of Missouri in the late 19th century. Old Drum was owned by a man named Charles Burden, a farmer with many fine hunting dogs. His brother-in-law, Leonidas Hornsby, owned a farm nearby. Hornsby struggled with stray dogs and other predators attacking his sheep, and he vowed to take revenge on the next dog he saw on his property. Unfortunately for Burden, that next dog happened to be Old Drum. Hornsby, or rather, his nephew, shot the hound dog on October 18, 1869, and subsequently lied to Burden about the unlucky pup's whereabouts. Burden took Hornsby to court. Burden hired a lawyer named George Graham Vest, who channeled the finesse of an Atticus Finch for fidos as he took to the courtroom floor. Vest eulogized Old Drum in an impassioned speech. Preaching to dog lovers everywhere, Vest sang the praises of our loyal canine companions, claiming that "when all other friends desert, [dogs] remain." The speech won the case, and $50, for Burden, turning the death of Old Drum into Missouri legend and Vest's winning argument into an anthem for dog lovers everywhere. In 2000, Old Drum's story was made into a made-for-TV movie called *The Trial of Old Drum*, starring Bobby Edner, Ron Perlman, Randy Travis, and a golden retriever as Old Drum.

Scientific Name: *Canis lupus familiaris* ("dog wolf of the household")

Order: Carnivora

Family: Canidae

Breed: Foxhound

Years: Died in 1869

Diet: Omnivorous (dog chow)

ON AUGUST 28, 2017, OLD DRUM WAS DESIGNATED THE STATE HISTORICAL DOG OF MISSOURI.

ANNA THE MEXICAN WOLF

Missouri has a long history of wildlife conservation. One of the most impressive organizations in the state is the Endangered Wolf Center (EWC), founded by Marlin and Carol Perkins in 1971. In its decades-long history, the EWC has played an important role in the breeding and reintroduction of several rare and endangered canid species, including Mexican wolves and American red wolves. Anna was a Mexican wolf, born on Earth Day in 2001. Her genetics were valuable—her father, Santa Ana, was one of the last pure Mexican wolves of his line. Anna had to be hand raised as a pup, meaning that she did not have the skills to be released into the wild. But in her nearly 14 years at the center, she played a tremendous role in the conservation of her species. Anna gave birth to 41 pups in four separate litters of record-breaking numbers. Several of her offspring now live in the wild. When National Geographic photographer Joel Sartore visited the EWC for his Photo Ark project, he was mesmerized by Anna and forever memorialized her with a portrait. Anna's image ended up on a US postage stamp, as well as being projected onto 33 stories of the Empire State Building in New York City. Anna also made an impression on the Perkinses' good friend Betty White. The two shared a memorable moment as Anna seemingly "showed" Betty her pups, inspiring the celebrity to kick-start a fundraising campaign that raised hundreds of thousands of dollars toward the EWC's important conservation efforts.

Scientific Name: *Canis lupus baileyi* (translates to "dog wolf" and named in honor of US government employee William Bailey, who collected wolf specimens)

Order: Carnivora

Family: Canidae

Status: Critically endangered as a subspecies

Region: Southwestern United States and northern Mexico

Diet: Carnivorous (small mammals and deer)

ANNA IS KNOWN AS THE "MATRIARCH OF MEXICAN WOLVES."

Photo by ©Joel Sartore/Photo Ark

PADDLEFISH HAVE SMOOTH SKIN WITHOUT SCALES.

PADDLEFISH

Missouri's state aquatic animal is the paddlefish. The paddlefish is a unique fish that historically lived in the Mississippi, Missouri, and Osage Rivers. It has a long rostrum that gives it a somewhat comical appearance. This fancy facial feature is thought to improve electroreception, helping the paddlefish to detect its prey. They typically swim slowly through the water with their gaping mouths wide open, eating tiny crustaceans and insects along the way. They are big fish, found at lengths up to five feet long and weighing more than 60 pounds. Scientists are interested in paddlefish because they are considered "living fossils." These fish are ancient, and their ancestors have been swimming on our planet for more than 120 million years. Sadly, the American paddlefish, which live here in Missouri, are the only surviving members of the Polyodontidae family. Originally, there were six species of paddlefish, including the Chinese paddlefish. The Chinese paddlefish was declared extinct in 2022 due to habitat destruction, and the other four disappeared from our planet a long time ago and can be found only in fossil records. We are so lucky to have an ancient fish like the paddlefish quite literally paddling through Missouri's river systems. But sadly, habitat destruction from human activity like levees and dams prevents paddlefish from moving upstream to their spawning territories. This means that paddlefish in Missouri can no longer reproduce on their own. Instead, they are hatched in human-run fisheries, and they are often overharvested. Hopefully, despite the challenges, creating healthy rivers for paddlefish to thrive will keep these fascinating creatures on our planet for another 100 million years.

Scientific Name: *Polyodon spathula* ("many-toothed spatula/blade")

Order: Acipenseriformes

Family: Polyodontidae

Status: Vulnerable and not self-sustaining

Region: Historically found in the Mississippi, Missouri, and Osage Rivers but now stocked in impoundments

Diet: Carnivorous (crustaceans, insects, and plankton)

CHANNEL CATFISH

The paddlefish may be Missouri's official state aquatic animal, but it is not the state fish. That honor goes to the channel catfish! It's a popular choice. The channel catfish is also the state fish of Kansas, Iowa, Nebraska, and Tennessee. One reason all of these states admire this fish? They're big, making them a great sport fish. Adult channel catfish can weigh up to 50 pounds. Catfish are called catfish because of their barbels. Barbels are the long, whiskery protrusions on either side of their face, which make them look like cats. Barbels are essentially whiskers for fish, serving the same role that whiskers do for mammals. They help the catfish to sense the world around them. Catfish tend to feed on a great variety of insects, crayfish, fish, mollusks, and plants at night. The barbels help the fish to locate their food in the darkness. Channel catfish can also communicate underwater with sound. These conversational critters will make sounds by clicking or grinding the pectoral fin bones within the pectoral girdle. This is called acoustic communication. The catfish uses it to help scare away predators or even attract a mate. Some have nicknamed the channel catfish the "swimming tongue" because of how many taste receptors cover their bodies. These receptors help the fish to navigate dark, murky water. They can even help the catfish to identify its friends just by taste!

Scientific Name: *Ictalurus punctatus* ("spotted fish cat")

Order: Siluriformes

Family: Ictaluridae

Status: Common

Region: Statewide

Diet: Omnivorous (fish, insects, crayfish, mollusks, and aquatic plants)

CHANNEL CATFISH ARE OPPORTUNISTIC AND HARDY, SURVIVING IN A VARIETY OF TEMPERATURES AND WATER CONDITIONS.

Photo by Chris Lukhaup/Missouri Department of Conservation

CRAYFISH

Have you ever been swimming in a lake or stream and been startled by a tiny, lobsterlike creature scuttling over your toes or seeking shelter under a rock? If you're in Missouri, then that was not a lobster. It was a crayfish! Crayfish go by many different names, depending on the region. Sometimes you will hear them called crawdads, freshwater lobsters, mudbugs, yabbies, or crawdaddies. There are around 600 species of crayfish in the world and 400 in North America. At least 38 unique species live in Missouri. That is almost 10 percent of the population found in the United States! The fact that we have so many types of crayfish in Missouri reflects the variety of aquatic landscapes in our state. Crayfish can be found in streams, swamps, marshes, lakes, burrows, or even underground. They are the largest invertebrate in Missouri. Invertebrates are animals that do not have a backbone. Instead they have an exoskeleton, a hard outer shell. Lots of different species eat invertebrates like crayfish. Crayfish provide food for more than 200 different species, including humans! You will often see them served in Cajun-style cooking, especially during Mardi Gras. Healthy water systems support thriving and diverse populations of animals like crayfish. So if you see one scuttling underfoot, count yourself lucky! You might just be wading in a clean stream.

Scientific Name: 38 different species in Missouri with the general name *Astacidea*, which means "type of crab"

Order: Decapoda

Family: Astacoidea

Status: 27 species are a species of concern in Missouri; others are prolific, farm-raised, or invasive in our state

Region: Statewide

Diet: Omnivorous (a wide variety of aquatic plants and animals)

WILD HORSES

Many Missourians are unaware that there is a herd of wild horses living right here in our state. The horses reside in Shannon County, in the southern part of Missouri, within the Ozark National Scenic Riverways. This land was set aside by the National Park Service to protect the area around the Current and Jacks Fork Rivers. One of the most magical parts of this park is the wild horses. These horses are said to be descendants of horses abandoned by their owners during the Great Depression as families moved out of the area in search of better economic security. But historical records going back to the 1700s mention the wild horses, implying that these animals have been a part of this area for several centuries. The herds of horses have not been without controversy. In 1990, the park superintendent decided that the horses should be removed because they are a non-native species. This argument made a lot of people mad because the horses are a well-loved addition to the area. Missouri's Wild Horse League soon formed, challenging the park service in court. Thousands of people protested the removal of the horses. As a result, the superintendent changed his mind. In 1995 the Ozark Wild Horses Protection Act was signed into law by President Bill Clinton, ensuring that Missouri's wild horses will always have a place in Shannon County to call home.

Scientific Name: Unknown; feral horses descended from domestic breeds

Order: Perissodactyla

Family: Equidae

Breed: Unknown

Diet: Herbivorous (grass, grain, and hay)

WILD HORSES ARE SOCIAL ANIMALS WITH A STRONG HERD HIERARCHY LED BY A DOMINANT MARE.

BALD EAGLES

The bald eagle is the national bird of the United States. You can't miss them, with their bright white heads, yellow beaks, and sharp "eagle eyes." Missouri and our neighbor Illinois have increasingly been perfect places to spot bald eagles. This is especially true in the colder months as they overwinter along the shores of the Mississippi River. But bald eagles were not always so common in our state. In the 1970s, bald eagles were on the Endangered Species List, thanks to a pesticide called DDT. DDT was used on crops and washed into the riverways, where it was absorbed by fish. Bald eagles ate those fish, with the unwanted side dish of DDT. DDT did not hurt the eagles. It just changed the way they processed calcium, so that when they laid their eggs, the shells were so thin and brittle they were crushed under the weight of their parents. With no way to consistently reproduce, bald eagle numbers plummeted. But don't worry. This story has a happy ending! In 1972, the Environmental Protection Agency (EPA) outlawed DDT. Over time, eagle numbers recovered, and today the International Union for Conservation of Nature (IUCN) lists them as a species of Least Concern, with numbers increasing nationally. So keep your eyes on the sky and your ears open for that signature screech. Your backyard may have the opportunity to play host to one of America's most spectacular species.

Scientific Name: *Haliaeetus leucocephalus* ("white-headed sea eagle")

Order: Accipitriformes

Family: Accipitridae

Status: Least concern worldwide but vulnerable in Missouri as an uncommon migrant

Region: Statewide near water in winter

Diet: Carnivorous (fish, carrion, small mammals, birds, reptiles, amphibians, and invertebrates)

BALD EAGLES HAVE EXCELLENT EYESIGHT AND CAN SPOT A FISH FROM MORE THAN A MILE AWAY!

PRAIRIE RACERUNNER LIZARDS

Missouri's ecosystem is home to a variety of rich habitats, such as glades! Glades are open spaces within forests. Missouri has several rocky glades, including in the Ozarks. These glades are like pockets of rocky desert, and they are the preferred habitat of the prairie racerunner lizard. In fact, racerunner lizards may be the most abundant reptile living within these glades. As their name implies, these lizards are fast. They can run up to 18 miles per hour! This skill is all in the pursuit of their favorite snacks—including invertebrates like insects, spiders, and scorpions. Talk about fast food! But the racerunner lizard is not all predator. They can also be prey. Good thing they have an insurance policy built right into their tails. When grasped by a predator, the racerunner lizard's tail breaks off, allowing this rapid reptile to escape. Like other lizards, the racerunner will eventually regrow its tail. Sounds like a pretty nifty party trick! Your best bet for spotting a racerunner lizard is to explore a sunny glade sometime between mid-April and mid-September. In the winter months, they like to burrow into the soil to escape the cold. As a bridge between the West and the East, Missouri is home to species from both sides of the United States. Our prairie racerunner lizards are a little taste of the Southwest, right here in the Midwest. Now that's something to be "glade" about!

Scientific Name: *Aspidoscelis sexlineatus viridis* ("shield-legged," "six-lined," and "green")

Order: Squamata

Family: Teiidae

Status: Common

Region: Southern Missouri and along the Mississippi and Missouri Rivers in northern Missouri

Diet: Carnivorous (a variety of invertebrates)

JUVENILES HAVE BRIGHT BLUE TAILS THAT FADE WITH AGE.

Photo by MH Herpetology/Wikimedia Commons
https://commons.wikimedia.org/wiki/File:Six-lined_racerunner_(Aspidoscelis_sexlineatus)_Madden_Haag.jpg

Photo by Lord Mountbatten/Wikimedia Commons
https://commons.wikimedia.org/w/index.php?curid=32556136

ALLIGATOR GAR ARE PRIMARILY NOCTURNAL AND CREPUSCULAR PREDATORS, MEANING THEY HUNT AT NIGHT OR DAWN AND DUSK.

ALLIGATOR GAR

In many ways, gar look like the stuff of nightmares. They resemble a fish crossed with either a bird or an alligator. Poking out of that long snout are several rows of sharp teeth. Missouri is home to four species of gar: the shortnose gar, the spotted gar, the longnose gar, and the alligator gar. The alligator gar is the largest. Alligator gar have a unique adaptation. They are covered in bony, tough scales called ganoid scales. Native Americans and early settlers repurposed these scales for arrowheads, breastplates, and coverings for tools. Alligator gar are not only the biggest but also the rarest in our state. They are a protected species, meaning that they cannot be fished in Missouri waterways. Habitat destruction and overfishing have caused their population to plummet. The Missouri Department of Conservation has worked to restock this species in areas around the Mississippi River for years. Though they may look scary, gar serve an important purpose in our ecosystem. They are one of the few fish that grow large enough to control invasive populations of Asian carp. Plus, these guys are survivors! They are a primitive species that's been on our planet since the Late Jurassic period. Now that's setting a high gar for success!

Scientific Name: *Atractosteus spatula* ("spindle-shaped bony spoon")

Order: Lepisosteiformes

Family: Lepisosteidae

Status: In Missouri a species of concern, critically imperiled

Region: Historically found in the Mississippi River as far upstream as the Illinois River, now declining

Diet: Carnivorous (fish and birds)

Photo by Greg Hume/Wikimedia Commons
https://commons.wikimedia.org/w/index.php?curid=93086899

Photo by fr0ggy5 on Unsplash

RACCOONS

If you've ever been outside at night in Missouri, you've probably seen a raccoon. Raccoons live all over our state, in rural, suburban, and urban landscapes. In fact, these little trash bandits are extremely successful at living alongside humans. Raccoons owe their success to their intelligence, agility, and rather indiscriminate dining habits. Yes, raccoons can and do eat trash. But they also eat wild fruits, grasses, nuts, crayfish, fish, snails, invertebrates, frogs, snakes, mice, eggs, squirrels, rabbits, and pretty much anything they can get their dexterous little hands on. Raccoons are well-known for their bandit-like masks and striped tails, but it's their hands that really make them special. Each hand has five fingers. They don't have opposable thumbs, but compared to other animals their hands seem quite "human." Raccoons use their hands to grip objects and wet their food. Scientists think that they're not actually washing their food but rather using the water to help their sensitive nerves learn more about what they're holding. Part of their scientific name actually translates to "the washer" as a result of this behavior! Aside from making creek water fondue, raccoons use their hands to help them climb. Whether they're scaling a tree to care for their babies in a nest cavity, or shimmying up a drainpipe to try to sneak into your attic, these adaptable animals get where they need to go!

RACOONS ARE INTELLIGENT PROBLEM-SOLVERS WHO CAN OPEN CONTAINERS, DOORS, AND LATCHES.

Scientific Name: *Procyon lotor* ("before dog" and "the washer")

Order: Carnivora

Family: Procyonidae

Status: Common

Region: Statewide

Diet: Omnivorous (pretty much anything!)

Photo by Richard Burton on Unsplash

PEANUT IS THE MASCOT FOR THE MISSOURI "NO MORE TRASH!" ANTI-LITTER CAMPAIGN.

Photo by Carolyn Mueller Kelly

PEANUT THE TURTLE

Peanut is a red-eared slider. Red-eared sliders are a common freshwater turtle in Missouri. But Peanut is anything but common. She's shaped like a figure eight! She wasn't born that way. Unfortunately, Peanut got her unique silhouette from a run-in with litter. When the Missouri Department of Conservation found Peanut in 1993, she had a plastic six-pack ring stuck around her middle. It's estimated that Peanut lived a full five years trapped in that ring. Over that time, the ring continued to squeeze her shell. Turtle shells are layered with malleable keratin (same as your fingernails!), resulting in Peanut becoming shaped like a popular legume. When conservation officers found her, they removed the six-pack ring and took her into human care at the Powder Valley Conservation Nature Center. There, guests can visit Peanut and watch her swim in her tank. Peanut is now in her 40s, but in the 30-plus years she's lived at Powder Valley she's led an incredibly impactful life. Peanut is a living example of what can happen to wildlife when humans are not being responsible with our environment. Luckily, Peanut is a survivor. But other turtles may not be so lucky. That's why we all must take on the challenge of keeping Missouri's wild places trash free.

Scientific Name: *Trachemys scripta elegans* (translates to the genus of pond turtle, "scripted" or "written" and "elegance")

Order: Testudines

Family: Emydidae

Status: Common

Region: Statewide

Diet: Omnivorous (aquatic plants, worms, insects, plant matter, fish, grasses, and snails)

BATS

Have you ever been sitting outside on a summer evening when, whoosh!, a bat dives through the air? Usually that first bat is followed by another, and then another. Don't be alarmed. Bats are not something to be scared of. They are amazing Missouri animals! In fact, they are the world's only flying mammal, which is pretty darn batty. There are around 14 species of bat in Missouri. The three most common are the big brown bat, the eastern red bat, and the evening bat. All of Missouri's bats are in the Vespertilionidae family. This means that they are fairly small, and they like to eat bugs. That's right. When they're swooping around your backyard, they're not trying to attack you, suck your blood, or get tangled in your hair. They are most likely out to do you a favor by chowing down on a flying mosquito buffet. A single big brown bat can eat up to 1,000 mosquitoes in an hour! When they are hunting, bats use echolocation to locate their prey. This means that they are able to emit sounds and then listen for the returning echoes to identify objects, like yummy mosquitoes. Bats are good moms too, paying extra attention to nursing, grooming, and caring for their pups. They're also long-lived, with some species living 30-plus years. So, get excited the next time you see bat wings gliding through the night. You've just spotted one of Missouri's most mesmerizing mammals.

Scientific Name (Evening Bat): *Nycticeius humeralis* ("belongs to the night" and "in the evening")

Order: Chiroptera

Family: Vespertilionidae

Status: Common statewide, though some of the 14 species are more common than others

Region: Statewide

Diet: Insectivorous (insects)

BAT PUPS DEVELOP QUICKLY AND CAN FLY WITHIN THREE TO SIX WEEKS.

Photo by Ann Froschauer/USFWS

Courtesy of National Park Service

NINE-BANDED ARMADILLO

What's one amazing Missouri mammal that doesn't look very mammal-like at all? The armadillo! Armadillos do meet the requirements of being a mammal. They are endothermic, or warm-blooded, they nurse their young, and they have hair. Armadillo hair is unique, though. It's found only on their bellies and between the hardened plates of skin that form to protect their back from predators. Many Missourians are familiar with armadillos as roadkill. Due to an unfortunate habit of leaping straight up when they are frightened, they are often hit by cars. These roadkill sightings have become more and more common in recent years, particularly in southern Missouri. Armadillos have moved further north in our changing climate. They prefer to dine on insects and other invertebrates. In the cold, winter months, these are less available. And unlike our amazing Missouri black bears, woodchucks, and turtle species, armadillos do not have a brumation period or hibernate. As the climate warms, armadillos are finding Missouri a more comfortable home and have become widespread, especially south of the Missouri River. We want to make these little critters feel welcome by watching carefully for them on roads, especially at nighttime since these tiny tanks are nocturnal.

Scientific Name: *Dasypus novemcinctus* ("hairy foot" and "nine-banded")

Order: Cingulata

Family: Dasypodidae

Population: Common

Region: More common south of the Missouri River but found statewide except for the northernmost regions

Diet: Insectivorous (ants, beetles, flies and worms with occasional fruit, fungi, or reptiles)

THE NINE-BANDED ARMADILLO IS THE ONLY VERTEBRATE THAT GIVES BIRTH TO IDENTICAL QUADRUPLETS EVERY TIME.

WHERE TO VISIT AND LEARN ABOUT ANIMALS IN MISSOURI

Saint Louis Zoo
1 Government Dr., St. Louis
314-781-0900
stlzoo.org

Kansas City Zoo & Aquarium
6800 Zoo Dr., Kansas City
816-595-1234
kansascityzoo.org

Dickerson Park Zoo
1401 W Norton Rd., Springfield
417-864-1800
dickersonparkzoo.org

Endangered Wolf Center
6750 Tyson Valley Rd., Eureka
636-938-5900
endangeredwolfcenter.org

St. Louis Aquarium at Union Station
201 S 18th St., St. Louis
314-923-3900
stlouisaquarium.com

World Bird Sanctuary
125 Bald Eagle Ridge Rd., Valley Park
636-225-4390
worldbirdsanctuary.org

Lone Elk Park
1 Lone Elk Park Rd., St. Louis
314-615-4386
stlouiscountymo.gov/st-louis-county-departments/parks/find-a-park/lone-elk-park

Powder Valley Conservation Nature Center
11715 Cragwold Rd., Kirkwood
314-301-1500
mdc.mo.gov/discover-nature/places/powder-valley-conservation-nature-center

Johnny Morris' Wonders of Wildlife National Museum & Aquarium
500 W Sunshine St., Springfield
800-456-4812
wondersofwildlife.org

Suson Park Animal Farm
6073 Wells Rd., St. Louis
314-615-4386
stlouiscountymo.gov/st-louis-county-departments/parks/find-a-park/suson-park

Grant's Farm
7385 Grant Rd., St. Louis
314-843-1700
grantsfarm.com

Longmeadow Rescue Ranch
480 Josephs Rd., Union
636-583-8759
longmeadowrescueranch.org

Purina Farms
500 William Danforth Way, Gray Summit
888-688-7387
purina.com/purina-farms

Sophia M. Sachs Butterfly House
15050 Faust Park, Chesterfield
314-577-0888
missouribotanicalgarden.org/plan-your-visit/family-of-attractions/butterfly-house

Eagle Bluffs Conservation Area
Southwest edge of Columbia, near McBaine
573-815-7900
mdc.mo.gov/discover-nature/places/eagle-bluffs-conservation-area

Audubon Center at Riverlands
301 Riverlands Way, West Alton
636-899-0090
audubon.org/riverlands

Lakeside Nature Center
4701 E Gregory Blvd., Kansas City
816-513-8960
lakesidenaturecenter.org